# PHILADELPHIA

Text by
RICHARD DUNBAR

Photos by
ANDREA PISTOLESI

BONECHI

# INDEX

*Project:* Casa Editrice Bonechi
*Publication Manager:* Monica Bonechi
*Picture research:* Monica Bonechi
*Cover, Graphic design and Make-up:* Manuela Ranfagni
*Map:* Stefano Benini - Firenze
*Editing:* Anna Baldini

*Text:* Richard Dunbar

© Copyright by Casa Editrice Bonechi - Florence - Italy
E-mail: bonechi@bonechi.it - Internet: www.bonechi.it

*Photographs from archives of Casa Editrice Bonechi taken by Andrea Pistolesi.
Photographs on pages 6-7, 8/9, 30 above, 32 below left, 39 below right, 42 above, 47 above, 50, 56 below, 60, 62 above right, taken by Jim McWilliams. Photographs on pages 24 above left, 27 above, 62 above left, taken by Arthur Wollock. Photographs on pages 4, 5, 13, 18-19, 19, were supplied by National Park Service Independence National Historical Park. Photographs on pages 54, 55, were supplied by Philadelphia Museum of Art.*

*The Publisher is grateful to
the Museum of American Art of the Pennsylvania Academy of the Fine Arts, Philadelphia for the permission granted to photograph the Academy interior, and to the Philadelphia Museum of Art for their kind cooperation.*

*Photos kindly supplied by Art Color Card Distributors: pages 14, 17, 22.*

ISBN 88-8029-926-3

* * *

# INTRODUCTION

Welcome to the United States' great historical city, where you can trace the steps of the most important figures of revolutionary America. Philadelphia is synonymous with the Declaration of Independence and the United States Constitution, with Independence Hall and the Liberty Bell, with Benjamin Franklin and Betsy Ross; but it offers much more than history. Philadelphia is also a young, vibrant city, with diverse and interesting neighborhoods, a flourishing arts scene, and hundreds of excellent restaurants. Still, Philadelphia's unique history cannot be ignored: it is visible everywhere, showcased in impeccable style.

Although Philadelphia has long been known as being conservative at heart, her origins represent a movement as radical as any for its time. Seventeenth-century England was not the place to be a religious radical, even if one's religion professed openness, non-violence and tolerance. Quakers, among others, were widely prosecuted, and even Philadelphia's Quaker founder and great espouser of religious freedom, William Penn, found himself imprisoned in the Tower of London at one point. Despite his brushes with the British Crown, this man of aristocratic lineage became the sole ''proprietor,'' at the age of 37, of an immense tract of rich, forest-covered land, generously watered by numerous rivers.

Pennsylvania–Penn wanted to call it New Wales, but the name meaning ''Penn's Woods'' was part of the deal–was a grant bestowed upon William Penn in 1681 by King Charles II, who had a £16,000 debt to settle with Penn's late father, Admiral Sir William Penn. William Jr. must have known a good deal when he saw it, and ever the religious idealist, he was quick to grasp the opportunity of founding his ''holy experiment,'' a place that would offer refuge to persecuted Europeans in search of religious freedom. Thus, Penn began laying down plans for Philadelphia, the City of Brotherly Love, where, in Penn's words, ''Ye shall be governed by laws of your own making and live [as] a free, and if you will, sober and industrious people.'' If that is not conservatively radical enough, then consider: ''No person shall be molested or prejudiced for his or her conscientious persuasion or practice. Nor shall he or she at any time be compelled to frequent or maintain any religious worship contrary to his or her mind .... '' These words, remarkable in their times, help to explain Philadelphia's rapid growth in its early years, as the influx of Europeans seeking religious freedom and new opportunities in the New World inevitably felt at home in this tolerant city.

The city that Penn envisioned, or at least parts of it, can still be visited today, as Philadelphia's predictable sys-

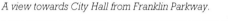
A view towards City Hall from Franklin Parkway.

William Penn
*(1644-1718)*
*British aristocrat, Quaker, religious free-thinker.*
*Founder of the city of Philadelphia.*

George Washington
*(1732-1799)*
*military leader, politician, first president of the United States.*
*Representative of Virginia at the congresses of Philadelphia.*

Benjamin Franklin
*(1706-1790)*
*writer, scientist, inventor, politician.*
*Drafter of the Declaration as the representative of Pennsylvania.*

tem of streets, laid out in a grid of right angles, was part of the founder's original plan. His "greene countrie towne," laid out by surveyor Thomas Holme, also included the five major squares that still grace downtown Philadelphia: Washington Square, Rittenhouse Square, Logan Circle, Franklin Square and City Hall. And when Penn sailed into fledgling Philadelphia for the first time in 1682, Holme was already there, preparing tracts of land for sale to settlers.

Also living there were the Lenni-Lenape, Native Americans who hunted, farmed and fished the rich lands and waters. Penn, it is said, was fairer in his dealings with the Indians than the white settlers in other colonies. Expecting to co-exist peacefully with the natives, he insisted that they be given a fair price for their lands, including for his own 8,000-acre estate. In the neighborhood today called Southwark, Penn also found a settlement of some 2,000 Swedes, whose 400-pound governor was known as Printz the Tub.

Penn remained in the New World for two years and when he left, many of the earliest settlers were still living in caves along the banks of the Delaware River. When he came back to Philadelphia in 1699 for his second and last time, Penn found a flourishing port town of 10,000 inhabitants, many of them living in brick houses packed in rows near the river. Penn's town had begun to take on a character of its own: it was less green than he had hoped, and instead of expanding neatly between the Delaware and Schuylkill Rivers, it remained intimately snug to the docks along the Delaware.

But if Philadelphia grew more haphazardly that its founding father had decreed, it was nevertheless industrious and, for the most part, tolerant. And this was enough to keep the newcomers flowing in and the city's stature rising. By the time a nearly penniless 17-year-old printer's apprentice arrived from Boston in 1723, Philadelphia was well on its way to becoming the colonies' largest, most important and most prosperous city. And its fortunes for the rest of the century, and beyond, would seem to be almost inseparable from the tireless energies and ideas of this young man. Printer, inventor, civic champion and statesman, Benjamin Franklin was to become Philadelphia's, and perhaps America's, best-known citizen during the heady decades that marked his 67 years in the City of Brotherly Love.

Franklin's role in making Philadelphia a city of firsts (subscription library, insurance company, fire company, militia, university, etc.), and second to London as the most important city in the English-speaking world, is perhaps only superseded by his contribution to American independence and the framing of the new country's constitution. Thus, although Philadelphia continued to grow and prosper into the 1760s, all was not well: in the opinion of many colonists, British rule had become too tyrannical and its taxes too arbitrary and punitive. And Philadelphia, founded on ideals of freedom instilled by William Penn, and with able statesmen like Franklin, was about to take center stage in the most significant events of American history.

Organized resistance and rebellion arose slowly but inexorably throughout the colonies in the 10 years between 1765 and 1774, when Philadelphia was chosen to host the First Continental Congress. Held in Carpenters' Hall, the Congress brought together delegates from the 13 colonies and resulted in a Declaration of Rights. Two years later, delegates would once again convene in a second congress, this time held in Independence Hall (then the Pennsylvania State House). This time, the delegates were no longer asking that

# IN CONGRESS, JULY 4, 1776.

## The unanimous Declaration of the thirteen united States of America.

their rights merely be respected: fighting had already broken out in Massachusetts, and the declaration they now issued demanded independence. George Washington was named the commander of all continental forces and Franklin, together with John Adams and Thomas Jefferson, were asked to draft a Declaration of Independence. On July 4, 1776, the delegates adopted the Declaration in the Assembly Room of Independence Hall, and on July 8, the bell that was later known as the Liberty Bell was rung to summon Philadelphians to Independence Square for a public reading of the Declaration. Franklin was sent as an envoy to France, where he deeply impressed the Parisians with his diplomatic skills and wit. He also managed to broker an all-important alliance with the French, who were instrumental in helping the Americans win the war. Philadelphia had weathered the war and British occupation (the Liberty Bell was carted off to Allentown to keep the British army from melting it down for ammunition). Now it remained to be seen if the city, and the rest of the new country, would be able to survive nationhood. The Articles of Confederation spelled out the "law of the land," but they were fast proving to be inadequate for exerting coherent rule over 13 non-cohesive states. At the urging of James Madison, the Constitutional Convention convened in Philadelphia in May, 1787. Once again, the city's Independence Hall was the focus of world attention. George Washington was named president of the convention, and, although some notables, like Thomas Jefferson, were serving diplomatic missions abroad, the group assembled there was lauded by some as the greatest gathering of statesmen ever seen. Chief among them were Benjamin Franklin, Alexander Hamilton and Madison, who was the principal drafter of the Constitution. It is indeed homage to these men that the United States Constitution, and the checks and balances of American governance that were worked out through negotiations and compromises during the convention, all continue to be very much alive today. As Franklin stated: "I consent to this Constitution because I expect no better, and because I am not sure this it is not the best."

In merely a century of existence, Philadelphia had already hosted enough momentous events to ensure its place in the pages of history books for innumerable generations to come. But, with hopes and expectations high at the threshold of the 19th century, the largest and most important city in the United States had no intention of slowing down. Already the country's leader in everything from industry to culture, it would vie to become the nation's capital, even though a site for the federal government had already been chosen on the banks of the Potomac River about 100 miles to the south. The government did reside in Philadelphia from 1790 to 1799, and city fathers tried to keep it there. But despite the considerable influence and wealth they possessed, Philadelphia's leading citizens had to resign themselves to seeing the U.S. Government take up res-

*A lone rower contemplates the skyline of Philadelphia.*

idence in the District of Columbia in 1800. The city didn't miss a beat as it entered the new century. In an increasingly industrialized world, Philadelphia stood at the forefront. It continued to be America's manufacturing and financial center, and coal arriving from the western part of the state fuelled new industries based on power from the steam-engine. At the same time, while culture continued to flourish, new cultures poured into the city to provide the manpower for the rapidly expanding industry. Between 1800 and 1860, Philadelphia's population grew eight-fold, from 70,000 to 565,000! And, as in other American cities, most of the impoverished multitudes arriving from Europe after 1820 did not have an easy time of it: they were overworked, forced to live in appalling conditions and targets of intolerance. And while the city was an important seat of the abolitionist movement–the American Anti-slavery Society was founded there in 1833 and the city was a major way-station in the Underground Railroad prior to the Civil War–tolerance of these movements was often in short supply. Following the Civil War–during which the city's 90,000 residents aided the Union Army, including 11 regiments of black soldiers–industry and commerce continued to grow apace. Although Philadelphia had since lost its primacy in some categories, such as commerce and population, to New York City, there was still no doubt of its place among the great and important cities of the world. Immense City Hall was under construction, though it would not be

ready for another of the city's crowning moments, the 1876 Centennial Exposition.

Increasingly, however, Philadelphia's history began converging with that of other large American cities. Still an industrial powerhouse, still wealthy, still Quaker at heart, the city rode the fortunes and misfortunes of the first half of the 20th century–two world wars punctuated by the great depression.

After joyfully celebrating the end of World War II, Philadelphia would have to take stock: industries were closing down or abandoning the city proper, as were hundreds of thousands of the city's residents. In their wake, Philadelphia found its treasures–where great moments of American history had not only been enacted, but had been written–hidden and crumbling among the vacant and dilapidated warehouses of the Old City. Likewise, the once elegant 18th-century homes of Society Hill housed one of the city's worst slums. Starting in the 1950s, Philadelphia embarked on a long and ambitious urban-renewal process, and today, much to the delight of residents and visitors, old Philadelphia shines like never before.

Yet, even as the city reaches back into its past, it looks into the future: the new energies flowing through the city have helped it shake off its stodgy image and made it into a flourishing center of arts and fine food. Indeed, at the turn of the millennium, Philadelphia seems poised to be a place of innovation once again–a familiar role for America's most historic city.

*Pages 8/9*
*The Benjamin Franklin Bridge and the skyline of Philadelphia.*

# OLD CITY

Philadelphia's **Old City** is often synonymous with **Independence National Historical Park**, and indeed is considered America's "most historic square mile." Within the colonial heart of Old City are contained Philadelphia's, and thus America's, most significant buildings and monuments, which provided the setting for many of the actions and words leading to the American Revolution and to the birth of a new nation. Old City also says something of modern Philadelphia and to the massive urban renewal efforts starting in the 1950s that were necessary to restore both the area within the Historical Park itself as well as the neighborhoods to the east of Independence Mall. In particular, these latter blocks, which contain such important sites as the **Christ Church** and cemetery, **Elfreth's Alley** and the **Betsy Ross House**, were filled with dilapidated warehouses before being transformed into a neighborhood of art galleries, converted iron-front warehouses and trendy apartments, restaurants and bars.

**Independence Hall** is, of course, where many of the most important acts and debates leading up to American independence and then the beginnings of American government took place. The name "Indepen-

dence Hall" was actually coined many years after those events, reflecting the role of the building between 1775 and 1800. Originally known as the **State House**, Independence Hall was built to house the Pennsylvania colonial government. Construction of the brick building, an outstanding example of Georgian architecture, began in 1732 under the direction of lawyer and amateur architect Andrew Hamilton and master carpenter Edmund Wooley. The tower of the building on the south side was completed in 1756. Finally, the steeple topping the bell-tower was erected in 1828 by William Strickland, replacing the unsteady original structure. The State House was eventually chosen to host the **Second Continental Congress** in 1775 (the first Congress was convened a year earlier and met in nearby **Carpenters' Hall**). On that occasion, delegations from the 13 colonies, responding to the first clashes of warfare breaking out in Massachusetts, gathered to organize local militias in the colonies so that they could stand up to the formidable British Army and to officially declare their intention to break with the motherland. Therefore, it was in the **Assembly Room** of the Pennsylvania State House that Virginian **George Washington** was cho-

*Independence Hall was the seat of some of the United States' most significant moments.*

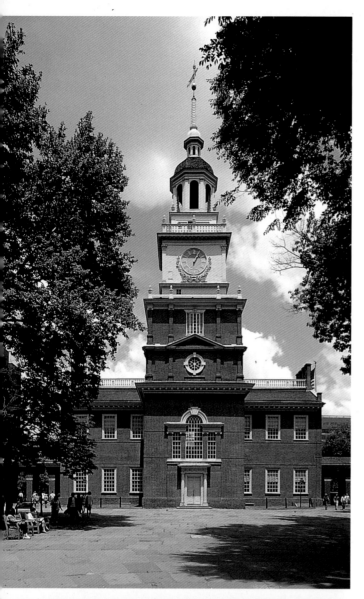

sen as Commander of "all continental forces," where **John Adams** introduced a resolution in which the colonies would reorganize as states, where **Richard Henry Lee** urged a resolution calling for independence, and where the **Declaration of Independence**, written mostly by **Thomas Jefferson**, was debated and, on **July 4, 1776**, adopted. Such momentous events would have been sufficient to ensure the building's place in history (although as we shall see, this was not almost the case); but the State House was to play host to other events that were arguably just as significant. In gaining independence, the first and most important step had been accomplished; but building and running a nation then had to be confronted. The **Articles of Confederation** had proved to be ineffective in holding together a growing and diverse nation, and the future shape of the form of government was left in the hands of the delegates to the **Constitutional Convention**, which met at the State House beginning in May, 1787.

With George Washington presiding over the convention, what was to become the **United States Constitution** began to take shape, and the famous document beginning "We the people ... " was sent to Congress four months later for ratification by the States. Despite the illustrious role played by the Philadelphia State House in American history, there was already talk of demolishing it at the time of Revolutionary War hero's **Marquis de Lafayette's** visit to the city in 1824. But Lafayette's evocation of the "hall of independence's" place in history not only helped inspire civic interest in restoring the structure, but it provided the building with a new name that has proven to be as resilient as the memories contained inside. The only way to see the inside of **Independence Hall** is by taking the half-hour walking tour conducted by Park Rangers and leaving about every 15 minutes from the Hall's East Wing. Among the sites visited are the **Pennsylvania Supreme Court Chamber** and the **Assembly Room**, where the most important events in Independence Hall took place. The **Syng Inkstand**, used to sign both the **Declaration of Independence** and the **United States Constitution**, is one of two original pieces in the Assembly Room. The other is the famous **Rising Sun Chair**. The Rising, occupied by **George Washington** during the Constitutional Convention, was made by Thomas Folwell in 1779. The chair received its name from **Benjamin Franklin**, the elder statesman of the Convention. When the delegates finally stepped forward to sign the Constitution after months of agonizing arguments and compromises had put the entire process in doubt, Franklin commented "now at length I have the happiness to know that it is a rising and not a setting sun."

*Two views of **Independence Hall**, from Independence Square.*

*The **Assembly Room**, above right, was where the Hall's most significant events took place and hosted some of the greatest statesmen living at the end of the 18th century, including **George Washington**, **Benjamin Franklin**, **Thomas Jefferson**, **John Adams**, **James Madison**, **Patrick Henry** and **Alexander Hamilton**. The **Supreme Court Chamber** was the meeting place of the Pennsylvania colony's highest court.*

13

# LIBERTY BELL PAVILION

The **Liberty Bell**, with its inscription "Proclaim Liberty throughout all the Land, unto all the Inhabitants thereof," is one of America's most enduring symbols. Those words, so fitting to the colonies' quest for independence, were actually intended to commemorate the 50th anniversary of William Penn's Charter of Privileges, responsible for making Pennsylvania one of the most tolerant lands in the world during that era. But the bell's popularity received its greatest boost in 1837, when it was adopted as the symbol for the antislavery movement and given the name "Liberty Bell." By the beginning of the 1900s, the Liberty Bell had traveled extensively in the United States, where throngs of visitors came to venerate it as a concrete representation of their country's origins. What is the first detail of the bell that inevitably comes to mind? Its crack, no doubt.

The Liberty Bell, in fact, hasn't rung since 1846, when in celebration of Washington's birthday the crack lengthened and widened, practically rendering the one-ton soundpiece useless. This bell is actually a recasting of the one ordered from Whitechapel Foundry in London in 1751 to celebrate the anniversary of Penn's charter. When the bell arrived in 1751, it either was received cracked or cracked shortly after arrival. Local brass founders John Pass and John Stow melted it down and recast it.

In June 1753 The State House bell rang for most important public events, including on July 8, 1776, when citizens were called to Independence Square to be informed of the signing of the **Declaration of Independence**. While no one is certain when the bell first cracked, it is was thought for many years that is occurred during the funeral of **Supreme Court Chief Justice John Marshall** in 1835, but that can not be substantiated. The centennial of American Independence in 1876 proved to be a boon for the popularity of the bell, and many souvenirs were made to commemorate it. One hundred years later, to mark the American Bicentennial, the bell was moved from Independence Hall to its present site in the glass-walled Liberty Bell Pavilion.

*The Signer Statue, left, is situated in the garden between Library Hall and the Second Bank of the United States. Library Hall, right, was the home of the colonies' first subscription library. This reconstruction, completed in 1959, now houses the library of the American Philosophical Society. The lovely facade is a faithful replica of the original.*

# LIBRARY HALL

One block to the east of **Independence Square** across 5th Street lies the historic Old City block containing **Library Hall** and the **Second Bank of the United States**. Both of these historic sites and the surrounding gardens are within **Independence National Historical Park**.

The facade of Library Hall is a replica of the Library Company of Philadelphia, which occupied the site between 1789 and 1884. The Library Company, which is now located at 13th and Locust Streets, was the first subscription library in the colonies and served as a kind of "Library of Congress" when Philadelphia was the seat of the U.S. Government. Members of the Continental and Federal Congresses and the Constitutional Convention used the Company's facilities, and the building served as the Library Company's headquarters until it was demolished in 1884. The original facade was the work of **William Thornton**, the architect who designed the **Capitol Building** in Washington D.C.

Library Hall was constructed in 1959 for the **American Philosophical Society**, and is an enlarged version of the original Library Company building. The Hall currently houses more than 200,000 volumes and manuscripts constituting the library of the Philosophical Society, including historically noteworthy first editions of Newton's *Principia* and Darwin's *Origin of Species*. It also holds documents written by Franklin and Jefferson, including a copy of the Declaration of Independence, William Penn's Charter of Privileges, and notes by Lewis and Clark. Although the library is used by scholars and researchers, a changing small exhibit of its collection is open to the public in the lobby.

# NATIONAL CONSTITUTION CENTER

The National Constitution Center, which opened to the public on July 4, 2003, is the Nation's first museum dedicated to celebrating and teaching about the U.S. Constitution. Groundbreaking ceremonies for this extraordinary building occurred on September 17, 2000, precisely 213 years to the day the U.S. Constitution was signed in Philadelphia. Located on the third block of Independence Mall close to the Liberty Bell and Independence Hall, the National Constitution Center is another reminder of the important role that Philadelphia played in the birth and development of America and its government. Visitors to the 160,000-square-foot National Constitution Center learn the story of the U.S. Constitution through high-tech exhibits, artifacts, and interactive displays. When entering the Center, visitors can see the flags of each of the states and U.S. territories, along with a huge, 12' x 18' American flag that has flown above each state and territorial capitol, and in Washington, D.C. The visit begins with a 17-minute multimedia presentation entitled **"Freedom Rising"** in the star-shaped Kimmel Theater, in which rousing music, live action and 360-degree images combine to tell the story of *We the People*. Following this experience, visitors enter the **DeVos Exhibit Hall**, in which multi-media interactive exhibits tell the story of the Constitution and of the civic responsibilities it requires. Circling the hall on the wall above is the entire text of the Constitution and all the amendments. In **Signers' Hall**, visitors can walk among life-size bronze statues of the 42 delegates to the Constitutional Convention present at the signing of the Constitution in Independence Hall. Stop and have your picture taken next to such luminaries as George Washington, James Madison and Benjamin Franklin, or become a delegate and choose to either sign today's Constitution or dissent. Just outside of Signers' Hall is one of the original public copies of the Constitution printed in a 1787 newspaper.

Among other activities offered at this new gem is the unique opportunity to take the Presidential oath of the office, wear judicial robes and rule on Supreme Court cases. In addition, lectures, performances and films about the Constitution periodically are available in the Annenberg Center for Education and Outreach. Don't miss the Llewellyn Citizens' Café, where visitors can watch government proceedings, obtain information on how to register to vote and e-mail elected officials...all just steps away from Independence Hall where it all began.

*The **National Constitution Center** is the Nation's first museum dedicated to celebrating and studying the U.S. Constitution*

*Following pages:*
*White steel frames mark the spot where **Benjamin Franklin**'s house stood. Franklin's "good House" was torn down in 1812 by Franklin's grandchildren, and plans of the structure were too incomplete to produce a faithful reproduction. **Franklin Court** contains the restored Market Street row houses.*

*Among Franklin's many vocations was that of a printer and newspaper editor. The printing equipment at **Franklin Court** is one of the many exhibits that attests to the life of this remarkable man.*

# FRANKLIN COURT

One of Philadelphia's most innovative monuments is that marking the home that **Benjamin Franklin** had built for himself in the courtyard–today called **Franklin Court**–off Market Street between 4th and 3rd Streets. White steel frames, designed by architect Robert Venturi and erected in 1976, show where Franklin's 10-room, three-story brick house was built between 1763 and 1786. It was, said Franklin, "a good House, contrived to my Mind." Unfortunately, the good house was torn down in 1812 by Franklin's grandchildren, and plans of the structure were too in-

complete to build a faithful reproduction. Franklin actually spent few years in semi-retirement in his house, having spent many years between 1763 and 1785 in Europe as ambassador to England and France. He returned to his house at the age of 80 and lived there until his death in 1790. The Franklin Court complex consists of four elements: the restored tenant buildings that Franklin had built on Market Street, a garden, the "ghost structures" representing the original house and his grandson's print shop, and an underground museum. The Market Street buildings, which

Franklin had built in the late 1780s and then rented out, have been restored and now house exhibits relating to some of the great man's contributions to society. Among his many talents, Franklin was known as a printer and as the country's first postmaster.

The **B. Free Franklin Post Office** is a functioning post office. Other buildings contain a reconstructed newspaper office (Franklin's grandson, **Benjamin Franklin Bache**, produced the *Aurora and General Advertiser* there) and 18th century printing and book-binding equipment. In yet another building, unfinished construction provides a look at fire-proofing methods invented by Franklin. A long ramp leads down to the underground museum, located beneath the Franklin's house. Among the exhibits focusing on the life and accomplishments of the great statesman, diplomat, inventor and civic organizer are displays of some of his inventions, such as the Franklin stove and the folding library chair and ladder. There is also an imaginative phone bank where you can hear what others, from **George Washington** to **D.H. Lawrence**, thought about one of the best-known men of his time.

# CARPENTERS' HALL

**Carpenters' Hall**, a block south of Franklin Court, is still owned and maintained by the **Carpenters' Company**, a trade guild founded in 1724 and the oldest building organization still in existence in America. Robert Smith designed the Hall, with construction beginning in 1770 and completed in 1773. His friend Benjamin Franklin moved his library into the building in 1773, the first lending library in the United States.

Both the Hall and the Carpenters' Company played important roles leading up to American independence. When the **First Continental Congress** was convened in Philadelphia in 1774 to allow delegates from the colonies to discuss their grievances with British rule, it was not clear in which direction the proceeding would turn. A more radical movement favoring independence, led by **John Adams**, had to devise a careful strategy to coax the more conservative elements. As part of this plan, the choice of the meeting place for the Congress was crucial. Conservative Tory-minded Pennsylvanian politicians, especially **Joseph Galloway**, Speaker of the Pennsylvania Assembly, attempted to exert influence over the Congress by holding the Congress at the Pennsylvania State House, now Independence Hall. But Adams and others favored a more neutral site, a privately owned building where their deliberations could proceed away from the conservative influence in Philadelphia, thus they chose Carpenters' Hall. While independence was not declared until the Second Congress, two years later, the debates and agreements set into motion in Carpenters' Hall were vital first steps towards creating consensus on the future of the colonies.

*Carpenters' Hall is still owned and maintained by the **Carpenters' Company**, the builders' guild founded in 1724. Both the Hall, completed in 1773, and the Company played important roles leading up to American independence. At the urging of the ''radical'' Company, which favored the colonies' break from Great Britain, the **First Continental Congress** chose to convene in the Hall in 1774, sending a clear message to the more conservative delegates who favored reconciliation with the British Crown.*

*The **Todd House** and the **Bishop White House,** facing page, provide two examples of the way Philadelphians lived at the end of the 1700s. The carefully tended 18th century formal garden between the houses is on the grounds of the **Pennsylvania Horticultural Society** (middle).*

# TODD AND BISHOP WHITE HOUSES

The **Todd House** and the **Bishop White House**, several doors from one another on Walnut Street, are two well-known residencies within **Independence Historical Park.**

Young lawyer **John Todd** lived with his wife **Dolly** in the brick row house dating from 1775 and typical of many middle-class homes constructed during the era. The modest furnishings, including John's law office, provide an accurate picture of the Todd's daily life. The couple lived here from 1791 until 1793, when John Todd fell victim to the yellow-fever epidemic that struck the city that year. Dolly married **James Madison**, who went on to become the country's fourth president.

In contrast to the Todds, **Reverend William White**, the first bishop of the **Episcopal Diocese of Pennsylvania**, lived in comparative opulence—he even had an indoor privy—as his larger and more ornate home suggests. The house in which the influential bishop resided from the time it was built in 1786 until his death in 1836 has been fully restored to its colonial elegance. White enjoyed the company of many of the nation's leading figures in his home, including **Washington**, **Jefferson** and **Franklin**.

*The new **Independence Visitor Center** is located directly across the street from the **Liberty Bell**, at 6th and Market Streets.*

# INDEPENDENCE VISITOR CENTER

The new Independence Visitor Center, located directly across the street from the Liberty Bell, at 6th and Market Streets, is the perfect place to begin a visit to the Philadelphia region. Patrons of the Visitors Center can get a peek at everything there is to do in Philadelphia's five county region, all in one place. At this one-stop destination, visitors can learn about new exhibits at museums and attractions, obtain information on the best restaurants and shopping spots; and make hotel arrangements for anywhere in the region. The Independence Visitor Center is the best place to learn details both about the area's many historic landmarks as well as help visitors discover the region's lesser known hidden treasures.

The Independence Visitor Center consists of 50,000 square feet of personal concierge and trip planning services, as well as reservation and ticketing services, including tickets to Independence Hall tours. The Center includes the National Park Service's revolving park exhibits that showcase items from the park's museum collection in addition to five permanent exhibits that focus on themes pertaining to Philadelphia and the birth of America. There are computer kiosks that highlight regional attractions, as well as several informational films that glow from the center's walls. This state of the art Visitor Center uses more than three miles of conduit to operate the audio-visual and trip planning displays! For more leisurely visit planning, read one of the many venue brochures in the coffee bar upstairs. The center is also boasts the **"Independence Store"**, one of the largest gift and book shops in the region.

# MERCHANT EXCHANGE

The **Merchant Exchange**, also called the **Philadelphia Exchange**, was built between 1832-33 in order to accommodate the burgeoning Philadelphia business community. This work of architect William Strickland, with its semi-circle Corinthian portico and elegant lantern, is considered one of the most beautiful examples of the Greek Revival style and a masterpiece of American architecture. The **Exchange Room**, which was located in the curved area, has a mosaic floor, a domed ceiling supported on marble columns and frescoes. The oldest stock exchange in the country, it was for 50 years a center of stock and commodity transactions, real estate dealing and auctions until it dissolved following the Civil War. Today it houses Park Service offices and is closed to the public.

*The colonial-era **Bond House**, above, is now a Bed & Breakfast operated by the National Park Service. Diners can still enjoy meals and drink in the **City Tavern** (middle and below right), once the haunt of America's forefathers. The **Merchant Exchange**, completed in 1833, is one of the most beautiful examples of the Greek Revival style and a masterpiece of American architecture.*

*Benjamin Franklin, George Washington and Betsy Ross worshipped in the **Christ Church**. Built between 1727 and 1754, the Anglican Church was considered the most sumptuous building in the colonies and one of the most outstanding examples of Georgian architecture. The Christ Church Cemetery contains the tombs of many of the city's luminaries, including **Benjamin Franklin**.*

# CHRIST CHURCH

Founded in 1695 as the Church of England, **Christ Church** is called the Nation's Church because many patriots, including George Washington, Benjamin Franklin and Betsy Ross, worshipped in this beautiful Georgian structure, built between 1727 and 1754. Its 200-foot steeple was the tallest building in America for 102 years. This is where the Protestant Episcopal Church of the United States was organized in 1789 with Christ Church Rector William White as its first Presiding Bishop. The **Christ Church Burial Ground** at Fifth and Arch Streets contains the graves of Franklin and four other signers of the Declaration of Independence and more heroes of the Revolution than any other burial ground in America.

# HORSE-DRAWN CARRIAGES

 *Carriages like these once carried wealthy Philadelphians through these same streets of the Old City. Today, visitors can relax in these relics and take leisurely and informative tours though America's most historic square mile and Society Hill, one of the country's oldest and most elegant urban neighborhoods.*

# ELFRETH'S ALLEY

Sitting snugly in the northeast corner of Old City is **El-freth's Alley**, the oldest continuously inhabited street in the United States. The earliest houses, which have two-and-a-half stories, date from the 1720s, while the "newer" three-and-a-half story structures were built after the Revolutionary War. Today, the street preserves its late 18th century look and gives visitors an idea of the way many of Philadelphia's cobblestone streets, jammed with modest, narrow row houses, appeared during that period. The alley was created in 1703 (shortly after William Penn's second and last sojourn to the city he founded) and originally served as a cartway separating the land of two property owners. **Jeremiah Elfreth** was a blacksmith who built and rented out some of the houses on the alley. Most of the homes were occupied by craftsmen who set up shop on the first floor and lived on the second floor. With the exception of houses number 124 and number 126, the **Elfreth's Alley Museum Houses**, the homes are still private dwellings. However, some of the houses open up to visitors on the first weekend of June, when residents dress in colonial clothing for the Elfreth's Alley Days, and on one evening in December, when Christmas tours are conducted. In the older homes, the doorway leads directly into the parlor, and facades are characterized by pent eaves and simple exterior woodwork, doors and transoms. The larger houses built at the end of the century reflect the influence of the Federal style with stairs leading to doorways framed by pilasters and pediments. The outside mirrors on the second floor are "busybodies," which allowed the inhabitants to see who had come to call at the front door. The museum houses, built ca. 1750, are typical of the earlier homes. During the latter part of the 1700s number 124 was the home of two well known Windsor chair makers. The first floor contains a Windsor chair maker's shop and household artifacts. House number 126 depicts the life of two Mantua Makers (seamstresses). The dressmaking shop is on the first floor with a colonial kitchen at the rear. Bedrooms on the second floor are reached by a narrow winding staircase.

# FIREMAN'S HALL

A few steps away from Elfreth's Alley is **Fireman's Hall**, a fun and fitting museum in the city that **William Penn** swore would never be destroyed by fire–which had devastated London in 1666–and in which the colonies first fire brigade, the **Union Fire Company**, was founded by **Benjamin Franklin** in 1736.
This real firehouse, built in 1903 and since restored, is packed with every imaginable bit of firefighting equipment from the last two centuries. Visitors can follow the exhibits and learn the story of firefighting,

*Elfreth's Alley is the oldest continuously inhabited street in the United States, with the earliest houses dating from the 1720s. Still preserving its late 18th-century appearance, the Alley gives visitors an idea of the way many of Philadelphia's streets appeared during that period. The **Elfreth's Alley Museum**, below, with its period furniture, is the only house on Elfreth Alley open to the public.*

from the "water-in-the-bucket" method to more sophisticated 20th-century techniques. You can also check out the array of 19th- and 20th-century hand- and horse-drawn fire wagons in the Hall's high-ceilinged main room. Other displays include collections of axes, helmets, badges, ladders, pumps, uniforms, as well as the firemen's living quarters on the second floor.

# BETSY ROSS HOUSE

The **Betsy Ross House** is the colonial period home of Betsy Ross where she sewed the first flag of the United States of America. Through a short, self-guided tour of the house visitors learn the story of the home, and the intriguing life of its patroness. Although Betsy Ross is known for sewing the first flag, she is also a prime example of a middle class working woman during early American history.

The Betsy Ross House was purchased and opened to the public in 1898 by the American Flag House and Betsy Ross Memorial Association. The site was taken over by the City of Philadelphia in the 1930s and restored to its appearance during the 1970s by Atwater Kent. Today the site is managed by Historic Philadelphia, Inc., a small non-profit organization established by Mayor Rendell in 1994, dedicated to improving the historic district and promoting tourism in Philadelphia.

*Philadelphia was home to the colonies' first fire company, founded by Benjamin Franklin in 1736. **Fireman's Hall**, a museum housed in a 1903 firehouse, tells the story of two centuries of firefighting.*

*The **Betsy Ross House** contains memorabilia of the famous Quaker seamstress' life. The modest 18th-century house and garden is one of Philadelphia's most popular attractions.*

# PENN'S LANDING

The long stretch of waterfront known as **Penn's Landing** is where **William Penn** first set foot in the future Philadelphia, where the first settlers lived in caves dug into the riverbank, and where Penn's surveyor, **Thomas Holme**, began marking out land grants.

Penn's Landing represents an ambitious urban renewal project that was undertaken, amid controversy, starting in 1967. By that time, most shipping operations had moved downriver to the southern end of Philadelphia, leaving behind empty warehouses and decaying piers. These have now been replaced with walkways, docking areas for pleasure boats, and an amphitheater, the **Great Plaza**, where crowds gather to hear free concerts and attend festivals and celebrations.

Stretching over 37 acres from South Street to Vine Street, the riverfront park contains numerous sites, such as the **Columbus Monument**, which stands next to the **World Sculpture Garden**. The *USS Becuna* and the *USS Olympia*, berthed next to each other, are a short stroll away from the Great Plaza. The *Becuna* is a guppy-class submarine commissioned at the end of 1944 and pressed into service in the South Pacific on search-and-destroy missions. The submarine continued to see action until 1969.

Volunteer guides are World War II submarine veterans, who know best what it was like for 88 men to live for months at a time in these extremely cramped quarters. The *Olympia* was one of the country's first steel ships and is the only remaining vessel from the

Previous pages:

The **Delaware River** provides an impressive foreground to Philadelphia's fast-changing skyline. The city's rich history is intimately bound to its waterfront, as Philadelphia was for many years the colonies', and then America's, most important port. More recently, **Penn's Landing** has transformed the crumbling waterfront into one of the city's most popular attractions.

The **Columbus Monument**, the **USS Becuna** and **USS Olympia**, and **Independence Seaport Museum** are among the attractions of Penn's Landing.

The **Thomas H. Kean New Jersey State Museum** has become a major attraction on the banks of the Delaware.

A couple of blocks away from the waterfront, at Walnut and 2nd Streets, stands **Old Original Bookbinders Restaurant**, one of Philadelphia's most venerated dining halls. This landmark restaurant first occupied this site in 1865, and today boasts of three bars and seven dining rooms, all decorated with memorabilia. Photos attest to the many notables who have dined at Old Original Bookbinders, which continues to be a favorite haunt for politicians, athletes and celebrities.

*The uniquely illuminated **Benjamin Franklin Bridge** was once the longest suspension bridge in the world.*

Spanish-American War, during which it served as **Commodore George Dewey**'s flagship and led the assault on Manila Bay. Its last mission was in 1921, when it sailed from France to the U.S. with the remains of the Unknown Soldier. Aboard the restored ship you can see the sailors' cabins and the officers' staterooms, the boiler room, the galley and the gun batteries.

The **Independence Seaport Museum** traces Philadelphia's maritime history through more than 10,000 artifacts, such as navigational instruments, figureheads and models of boats and ships. Kids will want to operate the crane unloading a container ship in **Home Port: Philadelphia**, or fish off the indoor pier. This exhibit also features the integral role of the waterfront in the city's social and economic life–the port was the colonies' major entry point for immigrants during the 18th century.

The **Workshop on the Water** gives young people a chance to learn traditional boat-building techniques.

# BENJAMIN FRANKLIN BRIDGE

When the **Benjamin Franklin Bridge** was completed in 1926, connecting Philadelphia with Camden, New Jersey, across the Delaware River, its 1,750 foot main span made it the longest suspension bridge in the world. Designed by Paul Philippe Cret, the massive blue structure rising 150 feet above the Delaware is another characteristic landmark on the city skyline.

The bridge provides a great view, whether you're looking at it (particularly good from the Chestnut or Walnut Street overpass heading to Penn's Landing), or looking at the city and the waterfront as you stroll across its south-facing walkway. At night a computerized lighting system, set up in 1976 for the United States Bicentennial, illuminates the bridge beautifully, highlighting the suspension cables and the arching roadway, and flashing with passing trains.

# SOCIETY HILL

Strolling through the alleyways and among the 18th-century homes of charming **Society Hill**, one finds a pleasant urban neighborhood. These several square blocks in the heart of Philadelphia today resemble the pleasant milieu that it was during Colonial times, when craftsmen and merchants lived side-by-side with some of the city's wealthiest and most influential citizens. With the exception of **Head House Square**, Society Hill is still largely residential, and its inviting narrow cobblestone streets, hidden shaded courtyards and row after row of beautifully and faithfully restored houses make it one of the city's most rewarding, and relaxing, areas to visit.

Architect I.M. Pei's **Society Hill Towers**, while out of context with the low buildings in the rest of the neighborhood, are nonetheless emblematic of the transformation of Society Hill that began in the 1950s. These luxury apartments were completed in 1964. The Philadelphia Redevelopment Authority bought many of the old residences and sold them to private individuals, who had to agree to restore the houses. The suc-cessful urban renewal effort ensured that this lovely neighborhood, with America's largest concentration of 18th-century buildings, would be preserved.

An ideal approach into Society Hill – named after the **Free Society of Traders**, who had received the land from **William Penn** – is through the Rose Garden off Walnut Street between 5th and 4th Streets (behind the Second Bank of the U.S.). Proceed to the Magnolia Garden, and then to **Spruce Street**, where you will see many examples of buildings that have been lovingly restored, down to the smallest details like boot-scrapers, busybodies, brass door-knockers and chimney pots. As you continue exploring the numerous small streets and courtyards and the juxtaposition of homes–houses of modest origins mix easily with those built by the more well-to-do–you may want to visit the few homes open to the public, such as the **Powell House** on 3rd Street, or the **Hill-Physick-Keith House**, a free-standing mansion on 4th Street. Also on 4th Street is **St. Mary's Church**, the oldest Catholic Church in Philadelphia. (Thanks to William Penn's pol-

*Old Swedes' Church*, or Gloria Dei, is Philadelphia's oldest church, dating back to 1700.

*A Man Full of Trouble Tavern*, built in 1759, was many of such rough-and-tumble public houses that crowded the docksides of old Philadelphia. The tavern stands in the shadows of the *Society Hill Towers*, luxury apartments designed by architect I.M. Pei. The three highrises are in sharp contrast to the rest of *Society Hill*, America's largest concentration of 18th-century buildings.

*Head House Square* in Society Hill was a covered market created in 1745; the **Head House,** below, was a volunteer firehouse. The square is still a market and draws crowds with its street artists and fairs and festivals and its numerous restaurants, cafés and boutiques.

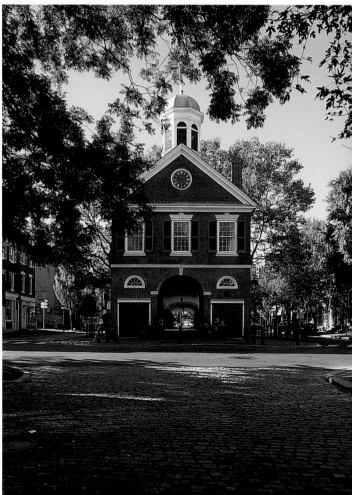

icy of religious freedom, Philadelphia was the only city in the British Empire where a Catholic mass could be legally performed.)

Sitting in the middle of **Head House Square**, which stretches for two blocks on 2nd Street between Pine and South Streets, is the covered Colonial market that was created in 1745. The brick building standing at the head of the market, **Head House**, dates from 1804 and was a volunteer firehouse. The square continues to be Society Hill's only shopping area and the neighborhood's most happening spot, drawing crowds with its street artists and fairs and festivals and its numerous restaurants, cafés and boutiques.

## ST. PETER'S CHURCH

As Philadelphia grew in the first half of the 18th century, the pews at **Christ Church** started overflowing with worshippers and a second church had to be planned. Therefore, as Christ Church continued to satisfy the needs of Old City residents, **St. Peter's Church** was built in the burgeoning area today called **Society Hill**. Opened in 1761, this Episcopal church designed by **Robert Smith** (who also designed Carpenters' Hall) has changed remarkably little over the ensuing years. Only the plain white steeple was added in 1852 by **William Strickland**.

The "chapel of ease," as St. Peter's was first called, still has high-backed pews raised off the floor to keep out drafts, and the unusual original design in which the pulpit and altar stand at opposite sides of the main aisle has remained unaltered. The church grounds complete the overall serene and typically 18th-century feel of the church. You can walk among the weathered tombstones, some of which mark the graves of Revolutionary War figures. Among those buried there are painter **Charles Willson Peale**, John Nixon, who made the famous first public reading of the Declaration of Independence on July 8, 1776, and the chiefs of seven Native American tribes who died in the yellow fever epidemic of 1793.

## DELANCEY STREET

From the Pine Street side of St. Peter's Church, you can walk towards **Delancey Street** by cutting through St. Peter's Way, which ends in front of shaded Delancey Park. This charming three-block-long street is one of Society Hill's most characteristic byways, even though individual or paired houses predominate here instead of the usual speculative row houses found in much of the other neighborhood streets. Especially noteworthy are the **Rhoads-Barclay** and **Trump** houses, and tiny **Drinker's Court**, with its small houses once rented out by the merchant who lived in the larger street-front home.

## SOUTH STREET

A few steps but a world apart from staid Society Hill is **South Street**, Philadelphia's hippest, most eclectic piece of real estate. Running from Front Street to about 9th Street, this stretch of road is jammed with hundreds of original shops, sidewalk cafés, eateries, bars and tattoo parlors and is typically transformed into a street fair–planned and spontaneous–in warm weather and on weekends. South Street is not a creation for out-of-towners and tourists looking for

*Opened in 1761 for Society Hill residents, St. Peter's Church, above, has changed remarkably little over the years. The "chapel of ease," as St. Peter's was first called, and its lovely grounds combine to provide a serene urban oasis in a typically 18th-century setting.*

*These two photos convey life on tree-shaded Delancey Street, which preserves some of the most characteristic homes in Society Hill.*

*Buzzing **South Street**, with dozens of original shops, sidewalk cafés, eateries and bars, is packed on weekends and evenings with people looking for a good time.*

*The chaotic **Italian Market** in South Philadelphia is the place to buy Italian cheeses, fresh pasta and other goodies.*

funspots in a colonial city; it is authentic, anchored by a local community that represents an easy mix of artists, merchants and workers. The southern boundary of William Penn's original city plan, South Street was home to a large Eastern European Jewish community in the late 1800s. But its present composition began to take shape in the 1950s, when many of the residents moved out to make way for a crosstown expressway, which happily never materialized.

# ITALIAN MARKET

**South Philly** is where most of the city's Italian immigrants settled, and the **Italian Market**, with its outdoor stalls lining **9th Street** for six blocks, is as authentic an Italian market as exists anywhere outside of the old country. Don't expect to find chic displays and fancy boutiques here–this is the real thing, with neighborhood customers looking for the best deals and the freshest produce along the chaotic, noisy sidewalk. This is the place to buy Italian cheeses, fresh pasta, warm bread, and to see suckling pigs hanging in butchers' shops. If you really love crowds, then try to come on Saturday morning, when it seems that half of Philadelphia is doing its weekly shopping.

# WASHINGTON SQUARE

Adjacent to Independence Square lies **Washington Square**, one of the original five public spaces in William Penn's "greene countrie towne". Never quite close enough to the old heart of the city to be a major civic and residential area until the 1800s, Washington Square has had a checkered history, ranging from a mass burial ground to the center of the United States publishing industry. Today, the tree-shaded park provides an ideal oasis for taking a rest from touring the nearby Independence Historical Park and Society Hill. The eclectic and vibrant neighborhood known as **Washington Park West** is one of the most pleasant to walk around and discover in the city. The square is also bound by several buildings of major interest and is in the proximity of **Antique Row**, the **Mikveh Israel Cemetery** and the **Walnut Street Theater**. From its earliest times until about 1825, the park was mostly used as a cemetery, especially for vagrants. Sitting at the center of Washington Square is the **Tomb of the Unknown Soldiers of the Revolution**, paying homage to the more than 5,000 American and British soldiers buried there during the war. Later, it was used to bury hundreds of victims of the yellow fever epidemic that ravaged the city in 1793. But as the city expanded, the square received its present name in 1825, and within several decades the area had become a well-off residential neighborhood.

On the east side of the Square is the **Anthenaeum**, a private library built in 1814 by the association of the same name founded by **Benjamin Franklin**. One of Philadelphia's first brownstone constructions and a fine example of Italian Renaissance Revival, the Anthenaeum houses changing exhibits on the first floor which are open to visitors. It is also worth asking to see the elegant reading room.

On Walnut Street is the **Curtis Center**, the one-time home of the Curtis Publishing Company whose empire included the *Saturday Evening Post* and *Ladies' Home Journal*. Also on the Square are the former offices of Lea and Febiger, the country's oldest publishing house. Today, the building houses the **Marian Locks Gallery** of contemporary art.

*The **Tomb of the Unknown Soldiers of the Revolution** pays homage to the fallen of the Revolutionary War. More than 5,000 soldiers are buried in **Washington Square**. One of the five public grounds in William Penn's original city plan, Washington Square was for many years a cemetery before becoming one of Philadelphia's wealthiest neighborhoods in the middle of the 19th century.*

*Pennsylvania Hospital was the colonies' first hospital and the first place that modern surgery was performed in the United States. Today, the hospital is a modern medical center, although parts of the structure are set aside for visits.*

*At the beginning of the 19th century, cabinet-makers began settling on Pine Street and crafting some of the finest furniture being made in the United States. Today,* **Antique Row** *offers a vast array of objects, including first-rate 18th-century furniture.*

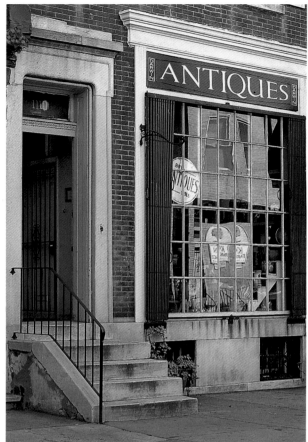

# PENNSYLVANIA HOSPITAL

**Pennsylvania Hospital** is not only one of the finest examples of Federal architecture in the United States, it was also the colonies' first hospital. It was founded by the eminent colonial physician, **Dr. Thomas Bond**, and the first portion of the hospital structure, the east wing, was completed in 1755, thanks also to fundraising efforts by **Benjamin Franklin**. The outstanding center section, built in 1804, is the work of **David Evans, Jr.** and shows the emerging sophistication in the design of public buildings. The domed amphitheater atop the central structure marks the country's first modern surgical theater. Today, the hospital continues to be a modern medical center. Thirty-minute self-guided tours take you to the **History of Nursing Museum**, the **Historic Library of Pennsylvania Hospital**, and a picture gallery featuring **Benjamin West**'s painting *Christ Healing the Sick in the Temple.*

# ANTIQUE ROW

Philadelphia, with its long, rich history, is an obvious mecca for amateur and expert antique hunters. Although shops abound in various parts of the city, **Pine Street**, between 8th and 13th Streets (three blocks southwest of **Washington Square**), has the highest concentration and is justly known as **Antique Row**. This area's link with furnishings goes back to the beginning of the 19th century, when cabinet-makers moved in and began crafting some of the finest furniture being made in the United States.

## CITY HALL

Whatever one's opinion of it, nobody can miss Philadelphia's impressive, and impressively massive, **City Hall**, which rises from the center of William Penn's original town plan. Today, the country's largest municipal building is generally recognized, and deservedly so, as a great work of architecture and perhaps the finest example of Second Empire architecture in the country.

Begun in 1871 and completed 30 years later, City Hall has 14.5 acres of floor space and more than 600 rooms, some of which are among the most lavish in the city. The ornate **City Council Chamber** is larger than the House of Lords in London; the **Mayor's Reception Room** has a blue and gold ceiling, mahogany panelling and faux finished red Egyptian marble columns; the **Council Caucus Room** is topped by a beautiful rotunda ceiling; and the recently restored **Conversation Hall** features granite walls and columns, mosaic floors and a magnificent chandelier.

On the outside, City Hall's pavilions, columns, and mansard roof blend in with **Alexander Milne Calder's** 250 statues that adorn the building. His best known statue, however, sits atop the tower (the world's tallest masonry structure without a steel frame): the 27-ton, 37-foot tall, bronze statue of **William Penn**, standing 548 feet above the city, is the largest piece of sculpture on any building in the world. The tower is open to the public and offers a spectacular view of the city.

*Claes Oldenburg's 54-foot high* **Clothespin** *stands in contrast with Philadelphia's* **City Hall***. The largest municipal building in the United States, City Hall is also one of the most impressive. The massive statue of* **William Penn** *standing more than 500 feet above* **Center City** *is the largest single piece of statuary to grace a building in the world.*

*The* **Pennsylvania Academy of the Fine Arts***, below right, is the country's oldest art school and museum, as well as architect Frank Furness' Victorian masterpiece.*

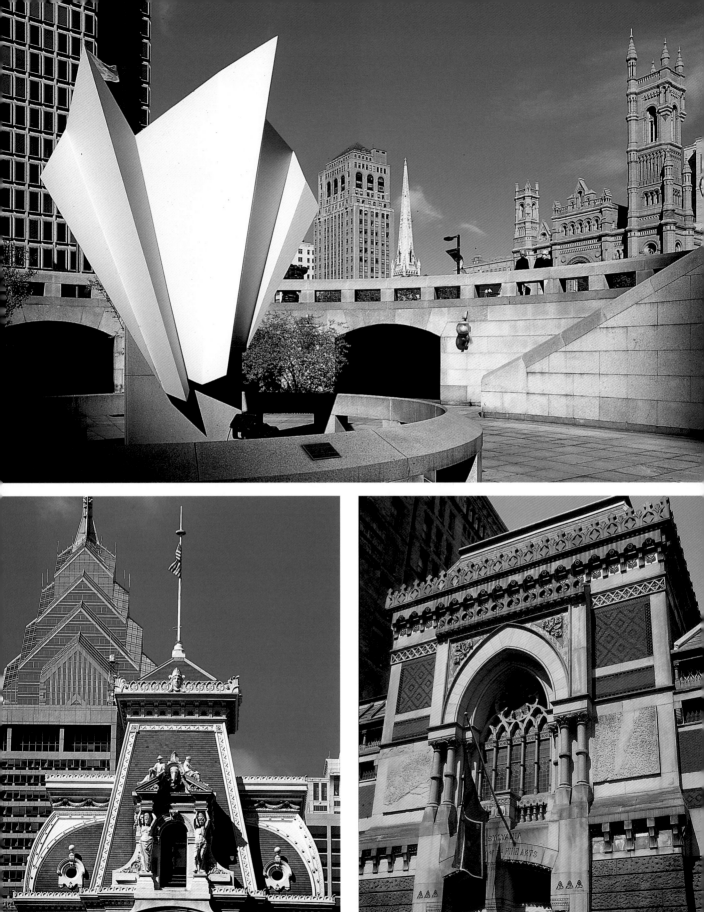

*Under the benign gaze of William Penn, **Broad Street** has some of Philadelphia's best architectural gems. The four blocks of Broad Street recently christened **Avenue of the Arts** is the place to go for theater, opera, dance and music.*

# BROAD STREET

The 12-mile long north-south running thoroughfare **Broad Street** is Philadelphia's grand avenue, graced with much of the city's finest architecture. Apart from **City Hall**, Broad Street is the home of the **Pennsylvania Academy of the Fine Arts**, the **Masonic Temple**, the **Girard Trust Company**, the **Land Title Building**, the **Union League** and the former **Bellevue-Stratford Hotel**. Starting from Locust Street, Broad Street encompasses the heart of Philadelphia's performing arts houses, and the four blocks between Locust and South Streets have been developed into the **Avenue of the Arts**. As the locus of the city's opera, dance, music and theater, all to be anchored by the planned new **Orchestra Hall** for the prestigious **Philadelphia Orchestra**, the Avenue represents an ambitious development project. Showing its faith in the project, the popular Wilma Theater, with its daring and progressive productions, has opened a new 300-seat theater on Avenue of the Arts.

At Broad and Locust, the venerable **Academy of Music** is the oldest concert hall in the country still in use. The lavish interior of the Academy, designed by architects **Napoleon LeBrun** and **Gustave Runge**, is modeled after La Scala opera house in Milan.

The **Mummers Parade** down **Broad Street** every New Year's day is a delightful Philadelphia tradition.

Love graces **John F. Kennedy Plaza**.

Public outdoor art flourishes in Philadelphia, as these sculptures next to City Hall demonstrate. The **Masonic Temple** on Broad Street (above) is one of the city's most impressive buildings, inside and out.

Joseph Brown's Benjamin Franklin, Craftsman pays tribute to Philadelphia's most famous citizen.

# AROUND CITY HALL

If one measure of civic pride is the amount of artwork that embellishes public spaces, then proud Philadelphia is second-to-none in the United States. The city has more outdoor works of art than any other city in the country, and the "1 percent rule," which sets aside 1 percent of all municipal construction costs for public art, helps Philadelphia maintain its reputation as a city that loves, and lives, its art.

In the plazas facing City Hall along 15th Street you can see this civic pride flourishing. And the many sculptures adorning the plazas once again prove that art is inevitably controversial and is not meant to please all of the people all of the time. **Claes Oldenburg**'s unmistakable **Clothespin** is a case in point (pictured on page 38). Some consider the Swedish-born artist's 54-foot high, 10-ton pop-art contrivance a welcome departure from the city's more traditional statuary. Others prefer tradition to towering steel clothespins. If you go to **Center Square Plaza** at 15th

BENJAMIN FRANKI

and Market Streets you can decide for yourself. The painted aluminum **Love Sculpture** in **John F. Kennedy Plaza**, at the beginning of the **Benjamin Franklin Parkway**, is familiar to many people. Since first appearing in a 1964 painting by Robert Indian, this peculiar design with the tilted "O" has been reproduced on numerous media, including a U.S. postage stamp. The sculpture was erected here in 1976 as part of the city's Bicentennial celebration.

As you stroll through these lovely plazas, affording extraordinary views of Center City around City Hall, the magnificent structure you come upon adjacent to City Hall on North Broad Street is the **Masonic Temple**, built between 1868 and 1873. The first meeting of the Freemasons in the colonies was in Philadelphia in 1732, and the brotherhood prospered during colonial times. The Temple was designed by 27-year-old Freemason, Brother James Windrim, who modelled it on the medieval Norman style. Once past the massive projecting carved wooden doorway, visitors can see the seven ornate and masterfully decorated Lodge halls, representing different styles of architecture: Oriental, Gothic, Ionic, Egyptian, Norman, Renaissance and Corinthian. The Masonic Museum features memorabilia of such historical figures as **George Washington**, **Andrew Jackson** and **Benjamin Franklin**.

*One Liberty Place made history when it was constructed at the end of the 1980s: it broke a long-standing "gentlemen's agreement" that no building in Philadelphia would rise higher than City Hall.*

*Benjamin West's* Death on the Pale Horse *is featured in the sumptuous museum of the* **Pennsylvania Academy of the Fine Arts,** *the country's oldest art school and architect* **Frank Furness'** *Victorian masterpiece.*

# LIBERTY PLACE TOWERS

The soaring tower at **One Liberty Place**, two blocks west of City Hall, would be noteworthy enough for its post-modernist look evoking the era of Art Deco sky-scrapers. But the real significance of the 960-feet high tower is that it broke the unwritten "gentlemen's agreement" that new buildings in tradition-loving Philadelphia would never surpass the gaze of William Penn, who stands atop City Hall. The project sparked heated controversy when it was proposed in 1987, but the developers prevailed and the city's skyline, and character, was irrevocably thrust into modern times. Today, most would agree that if the rule had to be broken, then it could not have been done so in a more excellent fashion than by this dramatic building. **One Liberty Place**, along with its slightly more staid twin at **Two Liberty Place**, is reminiscent of New York's Chrysler Building. The glass plated surface changes its hues with each passing hour and cloud, until it dominates the night-time skyline with its neon-trimmed edges.

# PENNSYLVANIA ACADEMY OF THE FINE ARTS

The **Pennsylvania Academy of the Fine Arts** is the country's oldest art school and museum, as well as architect **Frank Furness'** Victorian masterpiece. The interior and exterior of Furness' Broad Street building compete for the award of eclectic excellence, although much of its decorative brilliance only came to light after an extensive restoration in 1976.

The Broad Street site is the third one that the Academy has occupied since it was founded in 1805. Furness completed the structure in 1876, so that it could be unveiled for the Centennial celebrations. Among the museum's prize paintings is **Benjamin West**'s monumental, biblical *Death on the Pale Horse*. The self-taught painter from provincial Pennsylvania received formal academic education in Europe, where he went on to become a highly acclaimed artist. The Academy was so eager to add this work to its collection that it mortgaged its building to purchase it.

# CITY CENTER EAST

**City Center East** has for many years been known for its shopping, although retail slumps and shopping malls threatened to set this area into hard times several years back. Now, however, with new energy and money being pumped into these neighborhoods, you don't have to venture out of downtown Philadelphia when the shopping bug bites.

When **The Gallery** was completed in 1977 on Market Street midway between City Hall and Independence Mall, it was the first major retail building to appear in the city for more than 40 years. Extending over four city blocks, this popular mall, with its numerous shops, two major department stores, fountains, atriums and food courts, has become a favorite destination of city shoppers.

Further east, situated next to the Liberty Bell Pavilion in Independence Historical Park, **The Bourse** is a large 18th-century brownstone that was converted into a multi-level retail and office complex in 1982. This impressive structure once housed the city's maritime, stock and grain exchanges. Today, in addition to the numerous shops and eateries, The Bourse is also home to a theater/cabaret and supper club featuring live jazz performances.

*The Gallery and The Bourse have helped keep shoppers in downtown Philadelphia.*

Starting just north of Market Street, Philadelphia's **Chinatown** has been home to a Chinese community since the middle of the 19th century. Today, Chinese restaurants stand next to eateries featuring cooking from neighboring Asian countries. **Friendship Gate**, on 10th Street, is a colorful addition to the area. Completed in 1984, the gate was built by Chinese craftsmen and funded by Philadelphia and its sister city in China, Tianjin.

One of the key players in the area's renaissance is the new **Pennsylvania Convention Center**, which opened in 1993. Covering four city blocks, this daring venture to put Philadelphia high on the list of major convention venues is strategically placed. The majority of Philadelphia's most important and most frequently visited sites, as well as its major central shopping areas, are literally within short walking distance of the center. Two of the city's late 19th-century architectural gems are also part of the center. The ornate **Headhouse** of the **Reading Terminal** serves as the complex's entrance, while the terminal's great **Train Shed** is the center's grand hall. With a price tag of more than $500 million, the Convention Center is the most expensive construction project in the city's history.

The underground **Reading Terminal Market** pulses with life and is treasured by locals as a great place to eat and to buy the freshest food, many of it from local farms. Now partly beneath the Convention Center, the market became an immediate success when opened in 1892 one floor below the Reading Terminal. Although threatened with closure in the 1970s because of dropping business, the market today buzzes with activity as never before.

Among the many excellent eateries and food stalls in the market, some of the most popular are those run by Amish merchants from **Lancaster County**. If you can't make it to the Pennsylvania Dutch country, this is the place to sample their fresh breads, shoofly pie and scrapple.

*Friendship Gate* stands on 10th Street in **Chinatown**, home to an Asian community for more than a century.
Bustling **Reading Terminal Market** and the **Pennsylvania Convention Center** have helped revitalize the area known as City Center East.

# BENJAMIN FRANKLIN PARKWAY

Benjamin Franklin Parkway, connecting **City Hall** with the **Philadelphia Museum of Art** at the beginning of **Fairmount Park**, represented a bold diagonal statement through the regular grid plan of Penn's original city when it was laid out around 1920. Inspired by the City Beautiful movement, and by especially the Champs Élysées in Paris, the Parkway's designers, French-born architects **Jacques Gerber** and **Paul Philippe Cret**, saw this beautiful tree-lined boulevard, with its neo-classical buildings, statues and fountains as providing a welcome, and open, respite from the crowded city. The Parkway also concentrates many of the city's most important cultural institutions, including the **Free Library of Philadelphia**, the **Franklin Institute** and the **Rodin Museum**. It's about a 10-minute walk from **John F. Kennedy Plaza** at the Center City end of the Parkway to **Logan Circle**, named after James Logan, William Penn's agent and mayor of Philadelphia. Once a cemetery

*Alexander Stirling Calder's bronze figures look out on Logan Circle and Benjamin Franklin Parkway from Swann Memorial Fountain. The Parkway, connecting City Hall with the Philadelphia Museum of Art at the beginning of Fairmount Park, was inspired by the Champs Élysées in Paris.*

(and one of the city's original five squares), Logan Circle is now known especially for the **Swann Memorial Fountain** which emerges from its center. **Alexander Stirling Calder**'s three bronze figures stand for Philadelphia's three main rivers: the Delaware and Schuylkill Rivers and Wissahickon Creek.

As you approach **Logan Circle** from City Hall, the impressive Italian Renaissance style basilica on the right is the **Cathedral of Saints Peter and Paul**, the seat of Philadelphia's Roman Catholic Archdiocese. The Cathedral was built between 1846 and 1864, and is thus the only building on the Parkway that predates it.

On the other side of Logan Circle rises the **Franklin Institute Science Museum**, which opened in 1934. The Institute actually houses several museums specializing in interactive and hands-on exhibits, as well as a memorial to its namesake Benjamin Franklin.

Another impressive civic structure on the Parkway is the **Free Library of Philadelphia**. With over one million volumes, this centerpiece of the Philadelphia Library System is also known for its Rare Books Department, which can be visited.

About midway between Logan Circle and the Philadelphia Museum of Art, *The Thinker* and *The Gates of Hell* mark the entrance to the **Rodin Museum**, housing the largest and most important collection of Auguste Rodin's sculptures outside of France.

*Some of Philadelphia's most important cultural institutions are situated on tree-lined Franklin Parkway. The **Cathedral of Saints Peter and Paul**, left, is the only building on the Parkway that predates the boulevard. The **Franklin Institute Science Museum**, above, the **Free Library of Philadelphia**, middle, and the **Rodin Museum**, bottom, are located on the Parkway.*

*The world-renowned **Philadelphia Museum of Art**, with its superb collections covering a broad range of periods and continents, rises majestically at the end of the Benjamin Franklin Parkway. The bronze footsteps of Rocky's running shoes mark the end of the boxer's triumphant ascent up the stairs of the museum.*

# PHILADELPHIA MUSEUM OF ART

Sitting atop a hill called **Faire Mount** by William Penn, the **Philadelphia Museum of Art** is the crowning jewel of the Benjamin Franklin Parkway and, as it displays one of the country's greatest public collections of art, ensures the city's reputation as one of the major art centers of the United States.

Completed in 1928, the complex of three connected buildings modeled after Greek temples contains 200 galleries housing more than 300,000 works. Museum architect Horace Trumbauer's chief designer was Julian Abele, the first African-American graduate of the University of Pennsylvania's architecture school. After traveling to Greece to study temple architecture, Abele returned with the three-temple idea, part of which was incorporated into the present structure. In order to ensure that sufficient money would be found to complete the ambitious project, one of the museum's chief fund-raisers, Eli Kirk Price, suggested that work first be initiated on the two wings, which, he rightfully reckoned, leading citizens and civic leaders would not want to leave unconnected by the center temple. Although the museum can be entered from the parking area behind the building, the most re-

warding–and physically demanding–approach is from the front, where the Benjamin Franklin Parkway leads to a monumental flight of stairs flanked by cascading fountains. You may or may not want to run up the stairs as Rocky did, but when you get to the top and turn around you'll be rewarded with one of the best views of the green Parkway, with City Hall and the rest of Center City in the background.

Before entering the museum, stop and appreciate the three inter-connected temples, with tall porticoes and richly detailed pediments, set around the expansive terrace. The warm, golden hue of the facade derives from the use of Minnesota Mankato and Kosota stone, and the impressive gabled roof is covered with blue tile and crowned with bronze griffins. The glazed terra-cotta figures contained in the pediment of the north (right-facing) temple represents characters from classical mythology.

The museum's exhibit halls occupy the two top floors of the complex. As you climb the Great Stair Hall, you come face to face with Augustus Saint-Gauden's 1892 statue of the mythical huntress *Diana*. Apart from the section set aside for special exhibitions, the entire

*Augustus Saint-Gauden's statue* of the nude huntress Diana, above, greets visitors to the **Philadelphia Museum of Art**.

*Winter, an old man* and *Autumn, Bacchus holding a bowl*, both by Artist unknown, late 18th C, stone. In the background **Still Life with Hare and Birds** by Jan Weenix, late 17th C., oil on canvas.

*Bust of Benjamin Franklin* by Jean-Antoine Houdon, 1779, marble.

*Little Dancer of Fourteen Years* by Edgar Degas, after wax executed in 1880, bronze, tulle and silk.

first floor is dedicated to the museum's vast and impressive collections of 19th-century European art, early 20th-century art, American art and contemporary art. On the floor above, the John G. Johnson Collection covers Western art from the late medieval period to the 19th century.

The museum is notable because it contains important works of well-known artists over a broad range of periods. Among the most significant are the 15th-century *Saint Francis Receiving the Stigmata*, by Flemish master **John van Eyck**, and *Crucifixion with the Virgin and St. John*, by **Roger van der Weyden,** and considered one of the greatest masterpieces in American museums. Others include Reubens (*Prometheus Bound*), Vincent van Gogh (*Sunflowers*), Pierre Auguste Renoir (*The Bathers*), Paul Cézanne (*The Large Bathers*), Pablo Picasso (*Three Musicians*), Henri de Toulouse-Lautrec (*Bal at the Moulin-Rouge*), as well as paintings by Eugène Delacroix, John Turner, Henri Rousseau, Claude Monet, Paul Gauguin, Edgar Degas and Édouard Manet.

Modern works include those by such artists as Paul Klee, Constantine Brancusi (with the largest collection of his sculpture outside of Paris), Joan Miró, Salvador Dalí, Giorgio de Chirico and, more recently, Jasper Johns, Claes Oldernburg and Anselm Kiefer. **Marcel Duchamp** is the best represented artist here: don't miss his *Nude Descending a Staircase*, *The Bride Stripped Bare By Her Bachelors, Even*, and *Etant Donnés*. Works from the United States feature an important collection of art by African-American artists and by Thomas Eakins.

Non-Western works are also featured on the top floor in halls dedicated to Near Eastern and Asian art and to Japanese and Chinese art, while the Kienbusch Collection of Arms and Armor also appeals to children. Finally, the museum features rooms and structures packed up and shipped from various points in the world: don't miss the 12th-century French abbey, a Hindu temple from southern India with three 16th-century shrines to Vishnu, and a 14th-century Japanese *Temple of the Attainment of Happiness*.

*This collection of Greek style temples, called the **Waterworks**, once had the function of supplying Philadelphia with water from the Schuylkill River. Today they are one of many picturesque sites favored by visitors to **Fairmount Park**, the country's largest urban park. A few steps upriver from the Waterworks, the Victorian houses in **Boathouse Row** still host some of Philadelphia's rowing clubs.*

# FAIRMOUNT PARK

Philadelphians never tire of reminding visitors that their **Fairmount Park** is the largest piece of urban green in the United States. Their boast is well-placed–Fairmount Park contains an incredibly vast array of sites, including stately mansions, a wilderness gorge, a country inn, the Philadelphia Zoological Gardens and the only covered bridge remaining in a large American city.

The park is too big to explore on foot, making a bicycle, car or one of the Fairmount Park Trolley Buses run by the city a necessity for delving further into the green. But even those who are in a hurry can see two of the park's more famous areas. The picturesque collection of Greek temples on the banks of the Schuylkill behind the Philadelphia Museum of Art are the **Waterworks**, an esthetic solution for the city's need for water in the early 18th century. **Frederick Graff**'s Greek Revival buildings, now a National Historical Engineering

Landmark, covered steam engines that pumped millions of water per day to a reservoir on Faire Mount hill, where the Museum of Art stands today. From there, the water was gravity fed into the city. The pumping stations were modified over the years, reflecting technological advancements, but the Waterworks were finally forced to close down in 1909 when the Schuylkill became too polluted. Extensive restoration has been carried out to transform the Waterworks into an interpretative museum and restaurant.

A short walk upriver is **Boathouse Row**, ten Victorian buildings constructed in the late 19th and early 20th centuries. Outdoor lighting highlights the decorative details of the boathouses, creating an enchanting effect at night. Occupied by rowing clubs, known as the **Schuylkill Navy**, the boathouses have helped keep sculling a favorite sport in Philadelphia.

# SCHUYLKILL RIVER

The Delaware River and its port was Philadelphia's engine of commerce and trading link to the world; but much of the early wealth generated by that commerce ended up on the more idyllic **Schuylkill River**, as the numerous mansions and villas that grace parts of Fairmount Park attest to.

As the city grew, however, the towns popping up along the banks of the Schuylkill (this difficult to pronounce Dutch word means "hidden river") became increasingly industrial, and the river increasingly more polluted. But as the once vacant textile mills–now reconverted into offices and condominiums–on the banks of the Schuylkill in nearby Manayunk testify, the river doesn't pack the industrial might it used to. And now, more than ever, Philadelphians delight in strolling along, sitting beside, or rowing down their "hidden river."

The views along the winding roads on both sides of the river are enchanting. Especially on Kelly Drive, on the east bank of the Schuylkill, joggers, cyclists and walkers fill up the four miles of pavement on weekends, while collegiate sculling teams ply the water–all captured by the inevitable landscape artists, for which the river has long been a favorite model.

Behind the Philadelphia Museum of Art is the city at its photogenic best, with the Schuylkill River providing a backdrop for the impressive **Waterworks** and **Boathouse Row**. Visitors to the city in the month of May will see the river fill up with rowing teams from around the country competing in the Dad Vail Regatta. The river near the museum was further enhanced by the opening of the **Schuylkill River Park**, with its 1.25 mile-long path for bikers, runners and walkers and with stairways leading to the river.

The **Schuylkill River** runs placidly through the heart of Fairmount Park, offering spectacular views of Philadelphia. Roads and walkways along the river offer a tranquil respite from busy city streets.

*The **Japanese House and Garden** and the **Philadelphia Zoo** are among the major attraction of **Fairmount Park**.*

# MOUNT PLEASANT

Before becoming public domain, the lands comprising Fairmount Park were home to some of Philadelphia's wealthiest citizens. Many of the splendid villas and mansions they had built for themselves are open to the public. Foremost among these treasures is **Mount Pleasant**, which has the added trivia interest of being built by a pirate and being owned briefly by Benedict Arnold, America's most famous traitor.

**Captain John Macpherson** made his fortune as a legal pirate, sanctioned by the British Crown (they were called "privateers"), before settling in Philadelphia. The retired captain was an astute businessman and later became a farmer; he also had exquisite architectural taste, as his 1761 country estate demonstrates. **John Adams** called Mount Pleasant "the most elegant seat in Pennsylvania."

In 1779, when Macpherson could no longer afford to live in his mansion, **Benedict Arnold** bought it as a wedding present for his bride. But neither of them moved into Mount Pleasant, as Arnold was convicted of treason in the meantime.

# MEMORIAL HALL

One hundred years after playing such a major role in America's independence, Philadelphia was a logical choice for hosting a great celebration of the American Centennial. Maturing Fairmount Park was chosen as the venue for the **Centennial International Exposition**, which drew some 10 million visitors in 1876.

Of the grand buildings erected for the event (set on the west side of the Schuylkill River), only **Memorial Hall** remains, with its impressive huge green dome visible above the trees from numerous vantage points. Serving as the Centennial's Art Gallery, the Beaux Arts hall was designed by Hermann Schwartzmann, who had recently studied Beaux Arts in Vienna. Although Memorial Hall currently houses park offices, visitors can still view the spectacular main hall.

The **Smith Memorial Arch**, with its two Doric columns towering above Fairmount Park, marks the entrance to the Centennial grounds, even though it is a later addition completed in 1912. Built by the bequest of Richard Smith, a Civil War hero, the two triumphant arches are a war memorial, with two generals topping the giant columns, and statues of fighting men, including Smith, adorning the main structures.

*Mount Pleasant*, above, is one of the best known and most impressive of Fairmount Park's numerous mansions.

Built for the 1876 Centennial, Memorial Hall is one of Fairmount Park's more spectacular sites. The **Smith Memorial Arch** marks the entrance to the Centennial grounds.

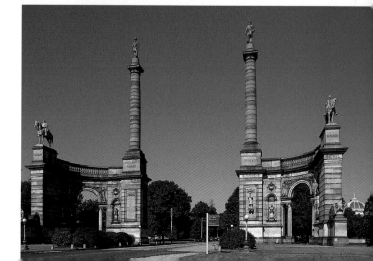

# UNIVERSITY CITY

The **University of Pennsylvania**, which with **Drexel University** gives this part of West Philadelphia its name, is a sprawling city campus covering 260 acres and serving more than 20,000 students. It was moved to this site in the 1870s, when its 9th Street Center City location was closed down.

The University is a direct offspring of the Academy, founded by **Benjamin Franklin** and other civic leaders in 1749 (its precursor, The Charity School, was founded in 1740 but closed down due to lack of funds). The Academy later became the College of Philadelphia and then, in 1779, the University of Pennsylvania, the nation's first university.

Another building you won't want to miss in University City is the **30th Street Station**, the country's second busiest railway station, and as majestic and monumental outside, with its great Corinthian columns, it is as warm and fascinating inside. The station, first opened in 1933, underwent a massive facelift in the early 1990s.

# VALLEY FORGE NATIONAL HISTORICAL PARK

The winter of 1777-78 was a crucial one for commander **George Washington** and his Continental troops. After suffering defeats to the advancing redcoats at Bandywine, White Horse and Germantown, the demoralized rebels fell back to **Valley Forge**, 20 miles from the center of Philadelphia, in December of 1777. Though lacking shelter, proper clothing, blankets and food, Washington's troops somehow managed to survive the fiercely cold winter months in their dismal encampment, albeit with a high toll in human life and suffering. Of the 12,000 troops that trudged into Valley Forge, 2,000 fell victim to disease and starvation. Today, although little remains of the desperate conditions in which the troops lived during that infamous winter, **Valley Forge National Historical Park** still provides a stirring look into one of the turning points in the War of Independence.

*Two students sit below the benevolent glance of Benjamin Franklin, on the **University of Pennsylvania** campus. Recently restored **30th Street Station**, above right, is one of the nation's most beautiful, and busiest, train stations.*

*Hundreds of log cabins like these had to be quickly built to protect the soldiers from the bitter cold in the winter of 1777-78. Despite heavy losses to disease brought on by the cold and hunger, Washington's troops emerged from their winter at **Valley Forge** as a strong and cohesive fighting unit. **Memorial Arch**, inscribed with tributes, pays homage to the men who braved the winter at Valley Forge.*

NAKED AND STARVING AS THEY ARE
WE CANNOT ENOUGH ADMIRE
THE INCOMPARABLE PATIENCE AND FIDELITY
OF THE SOLDIERY

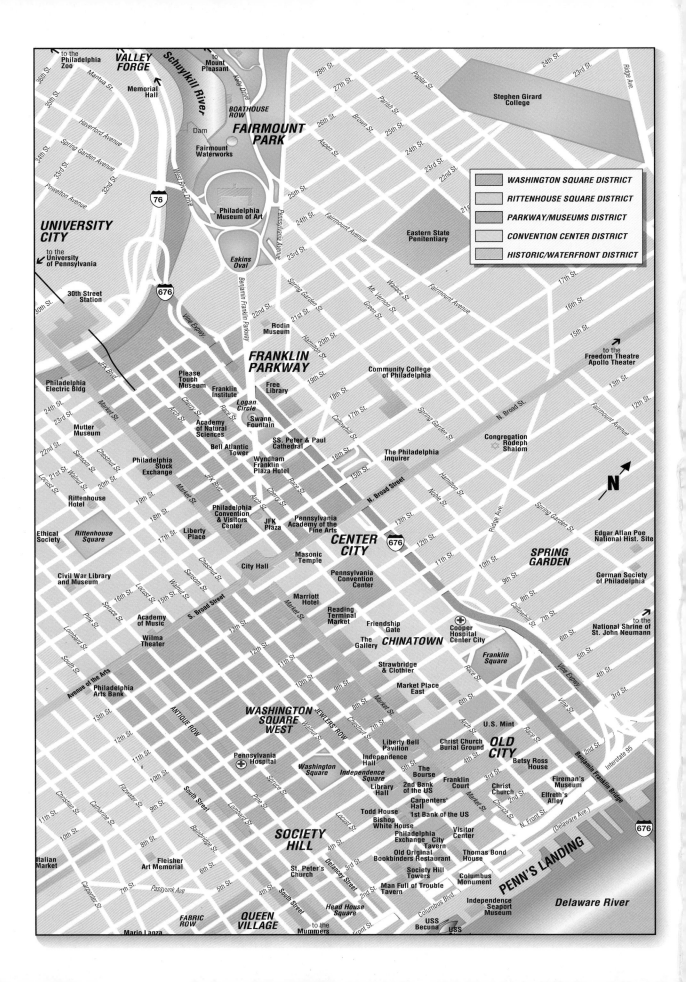